Hosta 'So Sweet' and Siberian Iris 'Lady Vanessa' compliment *Hakonechloa macra* 'Aureola'.

Left: 'Ferner Osten' and 'Blondo' Miscanthus have colorful fall flowers.

ornamental grasses add beauty and interest to the garden. Their dramatic change through the seasons gives a new dimension to the garden: an informal, natural look that is unique and refreshing. The objective of this bulletin is to publish the field research results from many grasses grown at four locations over 17 years in Minnesota. Information is included on culture, landscape features, and special uses of these grasses. This information should be useful to gardeners, nurseries, garden centers, landscape designers, and home-owners who live and garden in cold climates of the United States.

winter hardiness

Winter survival or hardiness information is based on research at the University of Minnesota, including multiple growing locations in USDA Zones 3 and 4. Illustration 1 (on page 4) shows the growing sites and years of field research. The grasses listed in this publication are hardy in USDA Zone 4, unless otherwise indicated. Plants that survived in USDA Zone 3 are listed on page 29. Although the research was conducted in Minnesota, this information is applicable to many states with similar climates from Maine to Montana.

culture and maintenance

Ornamental grasses can be planted in spring, summer, or fall. Spring planting represents the least risk and is the only time to plant bare rooted grasses. Supplemental water may be necessary for summer plantings. In the fall, plant only container plants with well-established root systems and allow for at least one month of growth before winter.

Determine spacing needs according to the desired landscape effect and the plant's setting. A good rule of thumb is to space plants equal to their mature height (plants 4' tall are spaced 4' apart), but you can plant further apart for specimen plants, or space plants one-half their height for a hedge or screen.

Division (digging the plant and cutting it into smaller sections, each with stem and roots) is the most common method of propagation. Named cultivars can only be increased by vegetative propagation and will not come true from seed. Some grasses can be propagated with stem cuttings, such as purple fountaingrass and miscanthus. Lower nodes on the stem are the most successful for cuttings. Seed propagation is typical for prairie restoration or for planting large areas where diversity is desirable.

Large mature grasses may benefit from spring division, especially if the center of the plant is dead. However, this may be a major job, requiring a strong back and a sharp spade. Division is not a requirement of grasses. Reasons to divide a plant include a need for more plants, an obvious dead center, or poor vigor. If you find a grass is declining and flowers are few, division may be helpful in rejuvenating the plant. *Calamagrostis xacutiflora* 'Karl Forester' can successfully be divided in the fall, but most other grasses respond best to spring division.

Cut back ornamental grasses to the ground to remove the previous year's growth. This should be done each year in late winter or early spring, before new growth starts. If the plants are not cut back, spring growth will be delayed and large plants will look unattractive and half dead throughout the year. Manual trimming with an electric hedge trimmer works well for

small areas. Large areas can be burned, if permitted and closely supervised. In this study, the grasses were burned to the ground, usually in early April. Some cool season grasses may be semi-evergreen such as *Deschampsia*, *Festuca*, and *Helictotrichon* and should be carefully cut back or any dead foliage and flowers removed with a rake or by hand. Burning cool season grasses should only be done when the plants are all brown and dormant. Do not cut back or burn any grasses in the fall as winter injury may result and the winter beauty of the plants is lost.

soil

In these field research plots, the soil pH varied from 7.2 to 7.8. Soils were loamy clays and glacial lakebed with high organic matter and water holding capacity. Many ornamental grasses will grow well on a wide variety of soils with a pH range of 5.0 to 8.0. Established grasses rarely need fertilization or irrigation except in cases of extreme drought or very sandy soils. In this research, organic wood chips were applied annually to prevent weeds.

pests

Hand weeding, or spot treatment with a contact herbicide for persistent weeds such as quackgrass was done in this study to eliminate weeds. Rust was occasionally noted on some species but no pesticide was applied and, other than weeds, no additional pests were noted on the plantings. Deer and rabbits had access to all these plantings, but no damage was noted.

features of grasses

- *Few insect or disease problems*

- *Low nutrient requirements*

- *Deer resistant—white tailed deer do not eat most ornamental grasses*

- *Little maintenance, except spring cutback*

- *More than one season of interest*

- *Fast growth—most are mature size by three years*

- *Varied texture, from fine fescues to coarse giant miscanthus*

- *An array of foliage colors from many shades of green to blue, yellow, bronze, and red, as well as several variegated forms*

- *Movement with the wind provides visual and audio interest; susurration that is pleasing and unique*

Above: movement in the wind is a unique attraction of grasses.

Center: Crookston, MN, zone 3.

Below: Morris, MN, zone 4.

cool and warm season grasses

Most grasses fall into cool or warm season growing patterns (see chart). Cool season grasses green up early in spring, produce flowers in late spring or early summer, may be dormant in summer especially in times of drought or high temperatures, and resume growth again in fall. Cool season grasses are often a contrasting two colors: green basal foliage and beige or tan flowers. Warm season grasses are slow to begin growth in the spring, flower in late summer and fall, grow actively in heat or summer conditions and are often drought tolerant. Growing both warm and cool season grasses will add a diversity of flowering times and interest in your garden.

Most grasses prefer full sun. These research plantings were in full sun, except for one section under shade at the Minnesota Landscape Arboretum. Grasses that tolerate shade and other special landscape uses are listed on pages 29-37.

cool and warm season grass growth chart

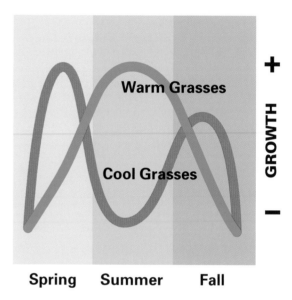

Warm Grasses

Cool Grasses

+

GROWTH

−

Spring   Summer   Fall

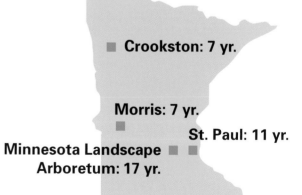

■ Crookston: 7 yr.

Morris: 7 yr.
■

St. Paul: 11 yr.

Minnesota Landscape ■ ■
Arboretum: 17 yr.

Illustration 1: Research locations and years of field hardiness trials. Morris, Crookston, 1996 - 2003; St. Paul, 1987 - 1998; Minnesota Landscape Arboretum, 1987 - continuing.

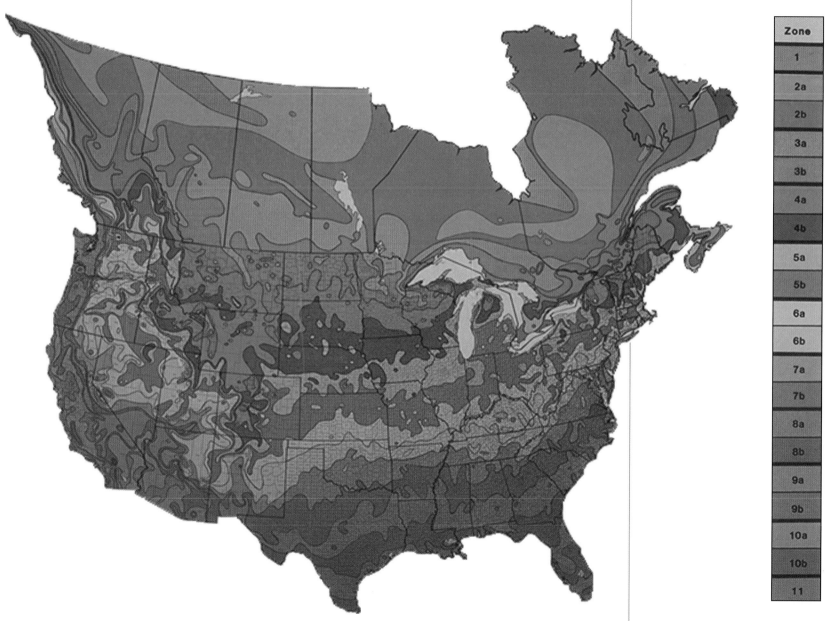

USDA plant hardiness map showing average minimum winter
temperatures. (Map courtesy U.S. National Arboretum, USDA-ARS.).

ornamental grasses from

Plants are listed alphabetically by botanical name. In addition to the common and botanical name, a pronunciation guide and some background on the meaning of the botanical name are included. (Please note that the ornamental grasses featured in this listing are hardy in USDA Zone 4 unless noted below.) Native location, cool or warm season, height, plant form, soil and site preferences are also listed.

yellow foxtail

yellow foxtail

Alopecurus pratensis   (al-o-pe-KEW-rus prah-TEN-sis)

alopec = foxtail, urus = looks like; pratensis = growing in meadows
Europe; cool season; 12-18″; dense clump; average soils; full sun

A European and American weed species, the yellow striped cultivar 'Variegatus' is the only form of meadow foxtail grown as an ornamental. Self-seeding has not been a problem. Grow in the front of a border and divide after several years to keep the plants vigorous. Grows best in cool weather and may decline in hot summers. Cut back in mid-summer to encourage new growth.

Cultivars:
❦ 'Variegatus' yellow foliage with green stripes

bulbous oatgrass

Arrhenatherum elatius
(ah-ren-A-the-rum el-AA-tee-us)

subspp. *bulbosum* 'Variegatum'
(bul-BOH-sum var-ee-uh-GAH-tum)

arren = male, ather = bristle; elatus = tall; bulbosum = bulbs
Europe; cool season; 12-30"; irregular clump; average to dry soils;
full sun to light shade

This can be a very striking white foliage plant, but declines in the heat of the summer and can be cut back at that time. The small bulbs or corms at the base of the plant can be used to propagate new plants. Benefits from frequent division. Good in containers and the front of a perennial border.

Cultivar.
'Variegatum', green and white foliage

Above: bulbous oatgrass. Below: sideoats grama.

side oats grama

Bouteloua curtipendula
(boo-tuh-LOW-ah kur-tih-PEN-dyoo-lah)

Bouteloua = C.& E. Boutelou, Spanish Botanists;
curti = side, pendula = peudulous
North America; warm season; 12-30"; upright-open; average to dry soils; full sun

A North American prairie native found on dry, upland sites although it will tolerate heavy clay soils. The pendulous flowers are often red when the stamens are shedding pollen. Grey-green foliage, typical of drought tolerant plants, is much shorter than the flowers. A tough plant for dry slopes and poor soils.

Above: blue grama. Below: 'Overdam' feather reedgrass.

blue grama

Bouteloua gracilis (boo-tuh-LOW-ah grah-SIL-us)

Bouteloua = after Spanish Botanists C.& E. Boutelou;
gracilis = slender, graceful

North America; warm season; 8-24"; irregular; average to dry soils; full sun

With minute "combs" for flowers, blue grama is ideal for dry soils and full sun conditions. It may self-seed. Great for dry prairies, atop septic mounds, or any dry sites. Can withstand heat, drought, mowing, and some foot traffic once established.

feather reedgrass

Calamagrostis xacutiflora
(kal-ah-mah-GROS-tis hybrid *ah-KYOO-tih-flor-ah)*

calam = reedlike, agrostis = grass; acuti = sharp pointed, flora = flowers

Europe; cool season; 4-5'; upright, narrow; average soils; full sun

Cultivars:

- 'Karl Foerster' is a very showy, upright, wheat-like plant that sets no seed and forms a dense clump. The pink flowers are short-lived in late spring, but the buff seedheads last till the next spring when the plants are cut back. Tolerates a wide variety of soils and may benefit from division, since the plants are so rapidly growing. Fits well in perennial plantings and is easy to grow. Named as the 2002 Perennial Plant of the Year.

- 'Overdam', a variegated selection that is 3-4' with fine, green and white striped foliage. Flowers are lighter, whiter than 'Karl Foerster' and resemble large astilbe flowers. Full sun, easy to grow, good for containers.

- 'Avalanche', a variegated form that has slightly wider foliage, is considered to be a reversion of 'Overdam'. Very stiff flowers, 3-4' tall.

fall blooming reedgrass

palm sedge, foreground; little bluestem, background

fall blooming reedgrass

Calamagrostis brachytricha
(kal-ah-mah-GROS-tis BRAK-ee-trik-ah)

calam = reedlike, agrostis = grass; brachy = short, tricha = hairs
Europe; warm season; 3-4'; upright-open; average soils; full sun

Pink to green flowers in September with an open, spreading vase shape. May lodge (fall over) and sparsely self-seed. Tolerant of a variety of soils and easy to grow.

Gray's sedge, mace sedge

Carex grayi (KAIR-x GRAY-eye)

carex = sedge; grayi = after American Botanist Asa Gray, (1810-1888)
North America; cool season; 2'; upright-open; average to wet soils; light to heavy shade

This native sedge grows best in shady conditions. The foliage will scorch in full sun even in Minnesota. Unique seedpods resemble a tiny medieval mace. The 1" wide foliage gives a bold texture in the garden.

palm sedge

Carex muskingumensis (KAIR-x mus-kin-goo-MEN-sis)

carex = sedge; muskingumensis = after the Muskingum River
Great Lakes of North America; cool season; 24-30"; upright-open; average to wet soils; full sun to medium shade

Native to wet areas along rivers and marshes, palm sedge is known for its stiff foliage and three-ranking leaf arrangement typical of sedges. The brown flowers are numerous in ideal sites with full sun. Easy to grow, tolerates standing water, at lake edges and soils that flood. Can grow to 30-36" wide, thick and full. Chartreuse foliage when grown in sun, dark green in shade.

Cultivars:
- 'Little Midge', very fine textured, 12-15" tall, stiff foliage
- 'Oehme' has yellow margins, slower growing, very attractive

Pennsylvania sedge

Pennsylvania sedge, sun sedge

Carex pensylvanica (KAIR-x PEN-sil-van-i-ka)

carex = sedge; pensylvanica = of Pennsylvania

North America; cool season; 6-12"; mound; average to dry soils;
full sun to heavy shade

Native to oak woods and dry sites, this fine textured grass-like sedge
will also grow in full sun, although the foliage may sun burn. Easy
to grow and may be used as a substitute lawn, will not tolerate foot
traffic, but forms a low mound less than 12".

Other sedges:

❧ *Carex buchananii,* leatherleaf sedge, not reliably hardy
   in zone 4, 2'

❧ *Carex comosa,* bottlebrush sedge, porcupine sedge, native to
   swamps, boggy areas, lake margins, 1-3'

❧ *Carex conica* 'Snowline', showy mound, large white mid stripe, may
   winter kill in zone 4, 12-14"

Carex siderosticha 'Variegata'

❧ *Carex flacca,* carnation sedge,
   blue sedge; vigorous
   rhizomes, low growing,
   glaucous foliage, 1'

❧ *Carex flagelifera,* 'Toffee Twist,'
   curly brown leaves, grow as
   annual, 12-15"

❧ *Carex lacustris,* lake sedge,
   native to bogs and lakes,
   tolerates standing water; 3-4'

❧ *Carex ornithopoda,* 'Variegata',
   showy, fine textured mound,
   8-10"

❧ *Carex siderosticha,* 'Variegata',
   hosta-like foliage 1 to 1-1/4"
   wide, 10-12" long, needs shade to prevent sunburn, 12-18"

❧ *Carex stricta,* tussock sedge, forms dense huge clumps in marshes
   and wet areas, 3-4'

northern seaoats

Chasmanthium latifolium
(chas-MAN-thee-um lat-ih-FOL-ee-im)

chasme = yawning/gaping, anthium = flowers; lati = wide, folium = leaves

Southeastern US; warm season; 3-4'; upright-open; moist to wet soils;
full sun to medium shade

May winter-kill in zone 4, re-seeds easily, especially in wet sites.
One of the best and most attractive grasses for cut flowers, does not
shatter when picked early. Chartreuse foliage on stiffer upright
plants when grown in full sun; in shade, the plants are more open,
nodding, darker green. Yellow fall foliage with bronze seedheads.
Native to rich woods.

tufted hairgrass

Deschampsia caespitosa
(deh-SHAMP-see-ah ses-pih-TOH-sah)

deschampsia = after L. Deschamps (1765-1842) French naturalist;
caespitosa = growing in clumps
Circumpolar No. Hemisphere; cool season; 3-4'; mound; moist to wet soils;
sun to shade

A native cool season grass found in moist woods in much of
the northern US. Usually requires moisture to establish. Semi-
evergreen, one of the first grasses to grow in the spring. Best
planted in mass where the flowers can make a cloud-like effect.

Cultivars:
- 'Bronzeschleier', bronze veil hairgrass, flowers are darker,
  more bronze colored
- 'Fairy's Joke', fairy's joke hairgrass, viviporous: small plants grow
  out of the seedpods and weight down the flowers
- 'Goldgehaenge', gold pendant hairgrass, yellow to gold flowers,
  very similar to 'Scottland'
- 'Northern Lights', foliage has white, pink, green, and yellow stripes,
  plants smaller, 12-18", slow growing, foliage may revert to green
- 'Scottland', Scotland hairgrass, yellow flowers

eastern bottlebrush grass

Elymus hystrix var. hystrix (Hystrix patula)
(ee-LYE-mus HYS-trix)

elymus = wild rye, a cereal; hystrix = bristly, porcupine-like
North America; cool season; 30-36"; upright narrow; average to moist soils;
full sun to heavy shade

Native to wooded areas in eastern and central US, bottlebrush can
be short-lived. Readily self-seeds. Foliage is chartreuse in full sun.
Attractive seedheads, but shatters readily. Good for wooded areas or
the edge of fields and prairies.

Above: northern seaoats. Below: tufted hairgrass.

Above left: fountaingrass and 'Elijah Blue' fescue with Heliotrope. Above right: *Hokonechloa macra* 'Aureola' with woodland *Phlox divaricata*. Below left: *Hakonechola macra*. Below left: blue oatgrass with *Heucherella* 'Bridget Bloom'.

sand lovegrass

Eragrostis trichodes (air-ah-GROS-tis tri-KOY-deez)

ero = love, agrositis = grass; trichodes = hairy
North America; warm season; 40-45"; mound; average to dry soils; full sun

A fine textured mound growing to 40" wide, with large red cloud-like flowers. May be short-lived, may self-seed. Marginally hardy in zone 4. The giant panicle makes an attractive cut flower, shatters with age. Along with *Eragrostis curvula*, these grasses are often planted on golf course roughs in the South and along highways for erosion control.

blue fescue

Festuca glauca (fes-TOO-ka GLOW-ka)

festuca = grass stalk; glauca = having bloom: a whitish powdery covering
Europe; cool season; 6-10"; mound; dry soils; full sun to light shade

These small mounds of silvery blue or blue-green spiky foliage fit well in a garden. Can be difficult to grow due to their requirement for well-drained soil and dislike of summer heat. Grow as annuals if you have heavy soil and hot summers. DO NOT BURN in spring; cutback carefully, or "comb" out the older brown leaves. Good in sandy, light soils. Easily self-seeds.

- 'Blaufink', blue finch fescue
- 'Blauglut', blue ember fescue
- 'Blausilber', blue silver fescue
- 'Boulder Blue', light silvery blue
- 'Daeumling', tom thumb fescue
- 'Elijah Blue', beautiful steel blue color
- 'Fruehlingsblau', spring blue fescue
- 'Harz', harz blue fescue
- 'Meerblau', ocean blue fescue
- 'Sea Urchin', sea urchin blue fescue
- 'Solling', solling blue fescue, few flowers, blue-green foliage
- 'Superba', superba blue fescue

hakone grass

Hakonechloa macra (hah-koh-neh-KLOH-ah MAK-rah)

hakone = from Hakone, Japan chloa = grass; macra = large
Japan; warm season; 12-20"; mound; moist soils; light to heavy shade

Native to moist, mountainous woods in Japan, hakone grass likes acidic soils that are moist with high organic matter. Prefers shade; slow growing. Can be wider than it is tall (to 25" wide), soft, weeping or pendulous, yellowish or olive green foliage; orange in the fall.

Cultivars:
- 'Albo-Striata', showy white striped foliage, 16-18" tall, 25" wide, soft weeping foliage
- 'Aureola', bright yellow foliage, 12-14" tall, 20" wide, slow growing

blue oatgrass

Helictotrichon sempervirens
(he-lik-toh-TRI-kon sem-per-VEYE-renz)

helix = spiral, trichos = a hair; sempervirens = evergreen
Mediterranean; cool season; 18-24"; mound; average to dry soils; full sun to light shade

Spiky, silvery blue foliage is attractive and combines well in a perennial border. Although it prefers drier, well-drained sites, and cool summers, it will grow in heavier soils. Late spring flowers are rare in the Midwest, oat-like and much taller, 36-40", than the foliage. Do not burn or cutback in spring; comb or rake out brown foliage.

Cultivars:
- 'Saphiresprudel', sapphire fountain, steel blue color

sweet grass

Hierochloa odorata (hee-ro-KLO-ah oh-door-AH-tah)

hieros = sacred, chloe = grass; odorata = fragrant
North America; cool season; 1-2'; irregular; average to wet soils; full sun

Sweetgrass is an irregular, unattractive grass, but the sweet fragrance of the foliage and flowers is long lasting and perfumes a room for months or years. A sacred ceremonial plant used by Indians for purification and memorial prayers, baskets, and smudging. Wonderful vanilla fragrance when dried. Rhizomatous, prefers wet soil, aggressive once established. Native to full sun and wet prairies in the Upper Midwest.

bloodgrass

Imperata 'Red Baron' *(im-per-AH-tah)*

Imperata = after Italian apothecary F. Imperato (1550-1625);
also imperial, royal, showy
Japan; warm season; 8-12"; upright-irregular; average soils; full sun

Showy red foliage. Can be difficult to establish and grow in zone 4; restricted in many states due to invasive nature of species from which this form is derived. Remove any green reversion plants, which are much more aggressive with persistent rhizomes.

silver hairgrass

Koeleria argentea (koh-LAIR-ee-ah ar-JEN-tee-ah)

Koeleria = after Botanist G. Koeler (1765-1806); argentea = silver
Europe; cool season; 8-12"; mound; average to dry soils; full sun

Yellow-green foliage with silver undersides, this short-lived grass likes well-drained soils. Greenish flowers turn brown with age.

sweetgrass

june grass

Koeleria macrantha (koh-LAIR-ee-ah mah-KRAN-tha)

Koeleria = after Botanist G. Koeler (1765-1806);
macra = large, antha = anthers
North America; cool season; 8-12"; mound; average to dry soils; full sun

Native to dry prairies, June grass flowers in the spring and has blue-grey foliage. Easy to grow, but may be short-lived. Good for septic mounds, dry gravely soils, and low-maintenance lawns. Can tolerate some foot traffic and mowing.

blue lymegrass

Leymus arenarius (LIE-mus air-hen-AIR-ee-us)
(synonym Elymus arenarius)

elymos = cereal; arenarius = growing in sand

Europe; cool season; 28-36"; irregular; average to dry soils; full sun to light shade

A vigorous plant known for growing on sand dunes along seashores but also grows well on heavy clay soils. Bright blue foliage and irregular growth habit. Good for erosion control. Flowers are sporadic. Tough and easy to grow, but persistent rhizomes may be too aggressive to control.

Cultivars:
'Blue Dune', attractive blue foliage

red melic

Melica altissima (MEL-ih-kah awl-TISS-ih-ma)

melike = sweet grass, (Greek); altissima = tallest

Europe; cool season; 30-45"; irregular; average to wet soils; full sun

Low foliage, 24-26", with taller, 40-45", dry, papery one-sided flowers; flowers June-August, readily self-seeds. Irregular growth habit, but showy flowers.

Cultivars:
- 'Atropurpurea', also sold in the trade as 'Red Spire', has red flowers that turn beige with age, flowers all summer but readily self-seeds.

Above: blue lymegrass. Below: red melic.

rubygrass

Melinis nerviglumis
(mel-EYE-nis ner-vee-GLUME-is)

meline = millet; nervi = nerves or veins, glumis = glumes (flower parts)

Africa; warm season; 20-28"; irregular; average to dry soils; full sun

Cultivars:
'Pink Crystals'™ is a 1998 Plant Select® introduction from the Denver Botanic Garden. Formerly known as *Rhynchelytrum repens,* this grass is not a perennial unless grown in frost-free climates. 'Pink Crystals' has a larger, thick seedhead, often nodding and pendulous. May self-seed. Tolerates drought and grows well in hot conditions.

Above: 'Pink Crystals' rubygrass. Below: *Miscanthus sacchariflourus* form a large rhizomatous clump.

silver banner grass

Miscanthus sacchariflorus
(mis-KANTH-us sa-ka-ri-FLOR-us)

miskos = stem, anthos = flower;
sacchariflorus = sugar flowers, flowers like sugar cane

Japan, East Asia; warm season; 5-6'; upright; average to wet soils; full sun

This rhizomatous species of *Miscanthus* is not recommended for gardens. The persistent rhizomes make it a permanent addition to the garden. Extremely hardy, USDA Zone 2, and early flowering (begins flowering in August), are good traits, but there are more attractive cultivars in the species *M. sinensis.* Plants in the Midwest set no seed. Can be controlled by regular mowing in the growing season or with a contact herbicide applied when plants are 12-24" tall. Very tolerant of wet sites, but native plants, such as *Spartina,* should be used for lakeshore stabilization.

japanese silvergrass

Miscanthus sinensis (mis-KANTH-us si-NEN-sis)

miskos = stem anthos = flower; sinensis = of China

Japan, East Asia; warm season; 4-8'; upright; average to wet soils; full sun

Many cultivars of this favorite grass are grown in gardens (see Table 1). The species is usually not seen in the trade and **SHOULD NOT BE PLANTED IN GARDENS.** The species (not cultivars) has escaped in mid-Atlantic states and can self-seed aggressively. Plant only named cultivars in garden settings where the plants can be watched for self-seeding. Usually, two or more cultivars are needed for cross pollination and seed set. *Miscanthus sinensis* and all cultivars are bunch grasses and form dense clumps. All cultivars prefer full sun and like moist soils. The tall plants are good screens and specimen plants in a perennial border. Flowers are showy, typical of Asia, and last well as cut flowers. Cultivars vary in height, flowering time, and hardiness (see page 20).

giant miscanthus

Miscanthus x 'Giganteus'
(mis-KANTH-us gye-GAN-tee-us)

miskos = stem, anthos = flower; giganteus = large size

natural hybrid; warm season; 6-11'; upright; average to wet soils; full sun

A large plant believed to be a natural cross between *M. sinensis* and *M. sacchariflorus* growing to 11 feet in zone 4. Hardy some years in zone 3, this plant makes an effective screen or maze. Children love it and try to hide inside the large canes. Researched extensively as a biomass fuel source in Europe, the huge canes are stiff and bamboo-like. Flowers late, in October. Wide foliage makes a pleasant susurration. Slowly creeping rhizomes, but not aggressive compared to *M. sacchariflorus*. Male sterile flowers and no seed viability.

'Giganteus' Miscanthus. The person shown is five feet tall.

miscanthus for cold climates

MISCANTHUS is one of the most popular ornamental grasses. Its showy, Asian flowers are tall and distinctive. In the US, there are three main kinds of Miscanthus, and it's important to be able to tell them apart. *Miscanthus sacchariflorus* has aggressive rhizomes. *Miscanthus x* 'Giganteus' is a giant plant that flowers in October. The third kind and most popular in the trade, *Miscanthus sinensis,* is a

plant only named cultivars of *Miscanthus sinensis* and only in managed landscapes where the plants can be watched for self-seeding

miscanthus sacchariflorus

- poor garden choice because of rhizomes, often seen on old homesteads in Midwest, control by mowing throughout the summer or a contact herbicide when plants are 12-24" tall
- aggressive rhizomes
- sets no seed in Midwest
- no awn on spikelet (see illustration)
- silky white hairs surrounding spikelet are 2-4 times the length of the spikelet
- all plants identical, soft white flowers in August/September
- excellent winter hardiness, USDA Zone 2

Miscanthus sacchariflorus— no awn extends from spikelet.

Above: 'Bitsy Ben', foreground, 'Rigoletto' and 'Zwergelefant' Miscanthus.

bunch grass with many garden cultivars (see pages 20-21). The species or "wild type" *Miscanthus sinensis* has become invasive in the mid-Atlantic states. If you grow more than one cultivar of *Miscanthus sinensis,* the plants may cross-pollinate and set seed. Plants should not be located where self-seeding can occur into an adjacent native woodland or prairie. Self-seeding was not a problem in this research, but all gardeners need to be aware of potentially invasive plants. Further information and illustrations on these pages will help you to know the different kinds of *Miscanthus.*

Miscanthus sinensis— awn extends from spikelet.

miscanthus sinensis

- plant only <u>named cultivars</u>, never the species which may self-seed and become invasive
- bunchgrass
- isolated plants set no seed, but two or more kinds can set seed: WATCH FOR SEEDLINGS
- awn extends from spikelet, and hairs surrounding it are equal to or shorter than spikelet
- wide variation in height, flower, and foliage color
- USDA Zone 4 variable winter hardiness

miscanthus x 'Giganteus'

- can grow to 11', makes a good screen, maze, or accent plant; thought to be a natural hybrid between *M. sinensis* and *M. sacchariflorus*
- slowly expanding
- male sterile, sets no seed to date
- awn extends from spikelet
- hairs surrounding the spikelet are equal to or shorter than the spikelet
- all plants identical, wide foliage and October flowers
- hardy in USDA Zone 4, some years in zone 3

what about pampasgrass?

Author with 'Herkules' (left), 'Roland' (background) Miscanthus.

Does Miscanthus look like what you call "pampasgrass"? In the upper Midwest, pampasgrass is a common name for Miscanthus. In the southern US, *Cortaderia selloana* is pampasgrass. In some catalogs, *Saccharum ravennae (Erianthus ravennae)* is pampasgrass. Common names alone can't tell you what a plant really is!

For more information, see the website Miscanthus Ornamental and Invasive Grass: *http://horticulture.coafes.umn. edu/miscanthus.*

miscanthus cultivar/species list

CULTIVAR OR SPECIES	FLOWERING* TIME	COLOR	HEIGHT	HARDINESS**	COMMENTS
M. floridulus	Early	not seen	8 – 9'	poor	not hardy; not grown in the US; tropical plant
M. x 'Giganteus'	Late	red	9 – 11'	excellent	1" wide foliage; October flowers; huge plant; slightly rhizomatous
M. oligostachyus	E	red-gold	4 – 4-1/2'	good	thin flowers; rhizomatous with age; yellow-green; shade tolerant
M. 'Purpurascens'	Mid	white-beige	5 – 5-1/2'	excellent	very hardy; drought sensitive; red-orange fall color
M. sacchariflorus	E	white	6'	excellent	invasive rhizomes; flowers fall apart early; in Midwest clones set no seed
M. sinensis var. condensatus	L	red-gold	6'	poor	1 – 2" leaves; a large plant native to coastal southern Japan; dense flowers
'Cabaret'	L	not seen	4'	poor	showy foliage; wide green center, white margins; grow as an annual
'Cosmopolitan'	L	not seen	4'	poor	showy foliage; wide white center with green margins; grow as an annual
M. transmorrisonensis	L	not seen	2 – 4'	poor	short; can be evergreen; tropical origin in Japan
M. sinensis cultivars:					
'Adagio'	M	pink-gold	3'	poor	fine–textured; short; similar to 'Yaku Jima'
'Autumn Light'	L	red	6'	fair–good	upright; showy duck-head red flowers
'Ben Uno'	E	beige	4-1/2 – 5-1/2'	good	low foliage; yellowish; not too showy
'Bitsy Ben'	E	red	4'	good	showy flowers; may develop rhizomes
'Blondo'	M	yellow-gold	6 – 6-1/2'	good	yellow foliage and stems; may lodge and self-seed
'Bluetenwunder' (flower wonder)	M	white-gold	6-1/2'	good	may lodge and self-seed
'Condensatus'	L	red	5 – 6'	poor	dense flowers, limited hardiness
'Dixieland'	L	red	5 – 5-1/2'	good	slightly shorter than 'Variegatus'
'Ferner Osten' (far east)	E	red	4 – 5'	good	showy flowers; medium- to fine-texture
'Flamingo'	E	white	5 – 5-1/2'	good	thick, pendulous; early flowers
'Goliath'	M	red	8 – 9'	good	huge and coarse-textured
'Gracillimus'	L	copper red	5 – 6'	fair	stiff and fine-textured; very graceful, but not fully hardy
'Graziella' (graceful)	M	white-gold	5 – 5-1/2'	good	showy flowers; good fall color
'Grosse Fontaene' (grand fountain)	L	red	5 – 6-1/2'	fair	chartreuse foliage; columnar; stiff
'Herkules'	M	white	5 – 5-1/2'	good	bright orange fall color
'Jailbird Ben'	L	red-gold	5 – 6'	fair	fewer bands than Zebrinus
'Juli' (July)	E	red-gold	5 – 6'	good	looks a lot like Malpartus
'Kaskade' (cascade)	L	pink-white	5 – 6'	poor	short-lived in zone 4
'Klein Fontaene' (little fountain)***	E	pink-white	5 – 5-1/2'	good	early, continually developing flowers; upright; medium texture
'Klein Silberspinne' (little sliver spider)	M	white-gold	4 – 4-1/2'	fair	small; fine-textured
'Kirk Alexander'	L	light red	5 – 5-1/2'	good	shorter; horizontal banding, but less than Zebrinus

CULTIVAR OR SPECIES	FLOWERING* TIME	COLOR	HEIGHT	HARDINESS**	COMMENTS
M. sinensis cultivars, continued:					
'Little Kitten'	L	not seen	12"	poor	very small; weak in zone 4
'Little Nicky' (Hinjo)	L	not seen	3'	fair	twice as many horizontal bands, but no hardiness
'Malepartus'	M	red	6'	good – excell.	large showy flowers; may self-seed
'Morning Light' ***	L	red	5 – 51/2'	fair	beautiful form and texture; October flowers; may winter-kill
'Mt. Washington'	M	yellow-beige	41/2 – 5'	good	foliage similar to 'Purpurascens'; purple fall color; MD seedling
'Nippon'	E	beige	5 – 5-1/2'	good	early flowers; red stems; may self-seed
'November Sunset'	M	red-gold	6 – 6-1/2'	fair	medium texture; may winter kill
'Positano'	M	red-gold	5 – 6'	good	medium height and texture
'Puenklchen'	L	red	5 – 5-1/2'	good	fewer bands/dots than 'Zebrinus'; shorter plant
'Rigoletto'	L	light red	5'	good	slightly shorter than 'Variegatus'
'Roland'	M	white-gold	7 – 8'	good	large and coarse-textured
'Rotsilber' (red silver) ***	M	red-silver	5 – 5-1/2'	good	very showy flowers
'Sarabande'	L	red	5'	fair	fine-textured
'Silberfeder' (silver feather)	M	yellow-gold	6 – 7'	good	slow to grow in spring; lodges; large and coarse-textured
'Silberpfeil' (silver arrow)	L	light red	5 – 5-1/2'	good – excell	very similar to 'Variegatus'
'Silberspinne' (silver spider)	M	red-gold	5 – 5-1/2'	good	fine-textured
'Silberturm' (silver tower)	L	white-gold	6 – 7'	good	lodges; coarse-textured
'Sirene'	M	dark red	5 – 5-1/2'	good	medium-textured; showy flowers
'Strictus', porcupine grass ***	L	red-yellow	5 – 6'	fair–good	stiff; columnar; shorter leaves and more banding than 'Zebrinus'
'Tiger Cub'	L	not seen	6 – 12"	poor	very small; weak in zone 4
'Undine'	M	golden red	5 – 5-1/2'	good	medium texture
'Variegatus' ***	L	red	5 – 6'	good	October flowers; may lodge when flowering
'Wetterfahne' (weather vane)	M	light red	5'	poor	short-lived in zone 4
'Yaku Jima'	M	not seen	2'	poor	short, fine-textured, but limited hardiness
'Zebrinus' ***	L	red	6 – 7'	fair–good	long leaves; bands appear in mid-summer; may lodge and self-seed
'Zwergelefant' (little elephant)	M	white-gold	7 – 8'	good	tall and coarse-textured

* FLOWERING TIMES: E= before August 15; M= August 15 – September 15; L= after September 15.
** WINTER HARDINESS DESIGNATIONS IN USDA ZONE 4:
    POOR: will live only 1 – 2 years; FAIR: will live 3 – 4 years; GOOD: will live 5 – 10 years; EXCELLENT: not limited by winter temperatures, hardy in USDA Zone 3.
***Voted as favorites by Master Gardeners and the public at the Minnesota Landscape Arboretum, 1995 – 2000.

Above left: variegated moorgrass. Above right: fountaingrass (foreground), tall purple moorgrass (back right).
Below left: 'Cloud 9' switchgrass. Below right: fall color, switchgrass 'Rotstrahlbusch'.

purple moorgrass

Molinia caerulea (moh-LIN-ee-ah ka-RULE-ee-ah)

Molinia = J. Molina, (1740-1829), Jesuit historian; caerulea = dark blue

British Isles, Europe; cool season with late flowers; 2-2 1/2'; upright, open or narrow; average to moist soils; full sun

Basal foliage with upright to upright arching flowers. Native to moors and bogs, prefers full sun. Grows best in cool summers.

Cultivars:
- 'Heidebraut', heather bride moorgrass, green flowers turning beige, 2-2 1/2'
- 'Moorhexe', moor witch moorgrass, dark green-purple flowers, upright narrow 2–2-1/2'
- 'Variegata', pendulous mound of yellow-stalked flowers and bright yellow-green foliage, 30-33" tall, 30-36" wide

tall purple moorgrass

Molinia caerulea subspecies arundinacea
(moh-LIN-ee-ah ka-RULE-ee-ah a-run-din-ACE-ee-ah)

Molinia = after Jesuit historian J. Molina, (1740-1829); caerulea = dark blue; arundinacea = resembling a reed

British Isles, Europe; cool season with late flowers; 5-7'; upright arching; average to wet soils; full sun

A tall, pencil-thin stemmed grass that adds height without weight. High, graceful stems sway in the breeze and are light and delicate. Several cultivars are quite similar, all with basal foliage at about 30-36" with tall elegant panicles that catch the wind and sun. Easy to grow in heavy clay soils, needs full sun and may self-seed. Grows best in cool summers. Flowers later than most cool season grasses. Yellow fall color, becomes prostrate in winter.

Cultivars:
- 'Bergfreund', mountain friend tall moorgrass
- 'Skyracer', skyracer tall moorgrass
- 'Staefa', Stafa (the Swiss city) tall moorgrass
- 'Transparent', transparent tall moorgrass
- 'Windspiel', windplay tall moorgrass

switchgrass

Panicum virgatum (PAH-ni-kum vir-GAH-tum)

panicum = millet; virgatum = twiggy, wand-like

North America; warm season; 3-6'; upright, upright-open; average to wet; full sun

A dominant grass in the tallgrass prairie of the central US, switchgrass is an aggressive, highly variable species. Will grow in standing water or ditches. Readily self-seeds and may dominate in a prairie or a garden. Winter cover and food for many birds. Good winter interest. Thick and full, may lodge (fall over). Large flowers are excellent for cutting. Grown from seed, plants will vary widely; named cultivars should be propagated by division.

Cultivars:
- 'Cloud Nine', upright arching to 6' or more, giant panicles, plant in the middle of a border with support for the huge flowers
- 'Dallas Blues', originated in Texas, large plant with 1" wide, blue foliage, large panicle whorls, good screen, limited hardiness, 5'
- 'Northwind', very stiff and upright, straight as an arrow, 5'
- 'Heavy Metal', upright, dense, thick foliage, 4-5'
- 'Prairie Sky', very blue foliage, lodges easily, can be prostrate by midsummer, 4-5'
- 'Rehbraun', red foliage and seeds, red-brown switchgrass, 3-4'
- 'Rotstrahlbusch', red foliage and seeds, red rays switchgrass (also know as 'Hanse Herms'), 4'
- 'Shenandoah', red foliage, shorter, 3-4'

fountaingrass

Pennisetum alopecuriodes
(pen-ny-SEE-tum al-oh -peck-yur-OY-deez)

penna = feather, seta = bristle; alopecu = foxtail iodes = looks like
Australia, East Asia; warm season; 3-4'; mound; average to wet soils; full sun

With attractive bottlebrush flowers, fountaingrass is hardy in zone 4, but often partially dies, leaving a lopsided, unsightly plant. Self-sowing has been a problem especially with seedlings that persist in mowed lawns. Prairie dropseed has a similar growth habit and may be a better choice for northern gardens.

Cultivars:
❦ 'Hameln', less likely to self-sow, 2–2-1/2'
❦ 'Little Bunny', very tiny, dwarf form, 6–8"

oriental fountaingrass

Pennisetum orientale (pen-ny-SEE-tum or-ee-en-TAL-ee)

penna = feather, seta = bristle; orientale = from the orient
Asia, India; warm season; 2–2-1/2'; mound to irregular; average soil; full sun

A more open, softer form of fountaingrass, with paler softer flowers, usually light pink to white. Flowers most of the summer. Has not been winter hardy in zone 4, but could easily be grown as an annual. Propagate by seed, which is usually apomictic: identical to the parent. Full sun.

crimson fountaingrass

Pennisetum setaceum (pen-ny-SEE-tum seh-TAY-see-um)

penna = feather, seta = bristle; setaceum = bristled
Ethiopia; warm season; 3-4'; upright arching; average to dry soils; full sun

Grown usually as a showy annual, crimson fountaingrass cannot tolerate cool temperatures or freezing conditions. Numerous attractive, long pink flowers; fine green foliage. In mild climates, can self-seed and becomes a roadside weed. Likes hot weather and can tolerate dry conditions. Good for containers and hot sites. Over-winter whole plants in a protected area; propagate by division and stem cuttings. Seed set is low, apomictic seed: all identical to parent.

Cultivars:
❦ 'Rubrum', purple fountaingrass, purple foliage and flowers, tender annual, sets no seed, no cold tolerance, likes heat, over-winter in a protected area, propagate by division or stem cuttings.

feathertop

Pennisetum villosum (pen-ny-SEE-tum vil-OH-sum)

penna = feather, seta = bristle; villosum = covered with hairs
Ethiopia; warm season; 2-3'; irregular;average soil; full sun

Weedy and irregular in juvenile growth, this tender perennial bears white-tufted flowers. Tolerates dry soils, likes hot climates and hot summers. Winter kills at freezing temperatures. May self-seed. Propagate by seed, apomictic: all seed is identical to parent.

Above: purple fountaingrass. Below: feathertop.

ribbongrass

Phalaris arundinacea 'Picta'
(fah-LAH-ris ah-run-din-AH-see-ah)

phalaris = grass; arundinacea = resembling a reed

Horticultural cultivar; cool season; 2-4'; irregular; wet to dry soils; sun to heavy shade

A tough, long-lasting garden plant that has been grown for centuries. 'Picta' means painted, referring to the striped leaves. The species (not the cultivar) is an extremely aggressive wetland plant, often growing in large monocultures. In the garden, ribbongrass tolerates almost any site and soil. Plant in sites where the rhizomes can be confined. Mow plants back in midsummer for a new flush of striped foliage.

Above: ribbongrass.

Cultivars:
❦ 'Feesey's Form', also known as 'Strawberries and Cream', is the best form to buy for the garden. Pink, yellow, and red-striped foliage, very showy in spring and easy to grow. Good in containers but even then may be too aggressive. Beautiful with other pastel colored flowers, 36" foliage, late spring flowers up to 50", may be sparse.

❦ var. *luteo-picta*, yellow ribbongrass, aggressive and becomes all green by midsummer when it can be cut back, 30-36"

little bluestem

Schizachyrium scoparium (synonym *Andropogon scoparius*)
(skits-ah-KEER-ee-um skoh-PAIR-ee-um)

**schizo = to divide, achuron (chaff) referring to the upper lemma;
scoparium = broomlike**

North America; warm season; 2-4'; upright; average to dry soils; full sun

A dominant of tall and shortgrass prairies, little bluestem is a common plant on mesic and dry sites. Variable in height and form, its blue foliage in the summer turns to a combination of purple, red, and orange in the fall. Grown as a forage plant for many years, the varieties 'Aldos', 'Little Camper', and 'Blaze' have been sold as seed-propagated selections known for creating a good stand for grazing and prairie restoration. 'Badlands' is a newer seed-propagated variety from the Dakotas. Little bluestem is an excellent grass for dry soils and difficult sites. Can readily self-seed, tough and easy to grow, especially on poor soils. Larva food for skipper butterflies.

Cultivars:
❧ 'The Blues', good blue color, may lodge (fall over), 2-3'

blue moorgrass

Sesleria caerulea (ses-LAIR-ee-ah sa-RUL-ee-ah)

Sesleria = L. Sesler, (1785) Italian Doctor; caerulea = dark blue

Europe; cool season; 6-12"; mound; average to moist soils; full sun

Glaucous blue foliage above, green on underside. Cool season grower, early to green up and flower. Small mound, similar to blue fescue, but much more tolerant of moist or clay soils, softer foliage.

Above: little bluestem, with feather reedgrass and sedum grow well on dry upland sites, high atop this lakeshore.

Indian grass

Sorghastrum nutans (sor-GAS-trum NOO-tans)

sorgh = sorghum, astrum = imitation; nutans = nodding

North America; warm season; 4-6'; upright; average soils; full sun

Common throughout the tallgrass prairie, Indian grass grows in medium moisture, or mesic soils. A dominate and easy-to-establish grass, and a backbone of prairie restorations. Showy flowers, often yellow from the numerous anthers, excellent as a fresh or dried cut flower. Named seed propagated varieties such as 'Holt', 'Osage', 'Oto', and 'Rumsey' have been selected for forage grasses with heavy foliage.

Cultivars:

❧ 'Sioux Blue', an excellent selection for gardens, tall, upright form, blue-green foliage, showy yellow flowers, 5–5-1/2'

Above: 'Sioux Blue' Indian grass. Below: cordgrass. Inset: *Spartina pectinata* 'Aureo-Marginata'.

cordgrass

Spartina pectinata (spar-TEE-nah peck-tin-AH-tah)

spartium = Spanish grass for weaving; pectinatus = comb-like

North America; warm season; 4-6'; irregular;
upright arching; average to wet soils; full sun

The slough grass of the prairie, found in ditches and wet soils, cordgrass has long, strap-like leaves and stout rhizomes. Excellent for erosion control along lakeshores and wetlands. Tolerates sandy seashores and heavy clay soils. Prefers full sun. Flowers are comb-like and coarse, not showy. In *The Long Winter*, Laura Ingalls Wilder twisted this grass to burn as fuel while awaiting spring on the prairie.

Cultivars:

❧ 'Aureo-Marginata', variegated cordgrass, yellow margins and stripes on the foliage, 4–6'

silver spikegrass

prairie dropseed

silver spikegrass

Spodiopogon sibiricus (spoh-dee-oh-POH-gon sy-BEER-i-kus)

spodios = ashen, pogon = beard; sibiricus = of Siberia

Siberia, Northern China; warm season; 3-4'; upright-open; average to wet soils; full sun

A dense, shrub-like grass with bamboo-like foliage. Hairy, ashen flowers that sparkle, sometimes called graybeard. Yellow, orange, or red fall color. Makes a thick screen or summer hedge. Weak stems easily break and prevent much winter interest. Grows best in cool conditions, likes moist soils.

prairie dropseed

Sporobolus heterolepis
(spor-AH-boh-lus het-er-oh-LEP-is)

spora = seed, ballein = to throw; heter = diversely, lepis = scaled

North America; warm season; 2–2 1/2'; mound; average to dry soils; full sun

A fine-textured mound common to dry prairie sites. Prairie dropseed is a beautiful grass with fine, light airy flowers. The round, bead-like seeds are oily and fall from the plant when ripe. Their fragrance is very characteristic, smelling like hot buttered popcorn or coriander and cumin. Easy to grow but may be slow to establish. Prefers dry, well-drained soils and spring propagation.

grasses for different landscape needs

water gardens, standing water, and along lakeshores

- *Acorus calamus* 'Variegatus', variegated sweet flag
- *Carex comosa*, bottlebrush sedge N
- *Carex muskingumensis*, palm sedge N
- *Carex stricta*, tussock sedge N
- *Chasmanthium latifolium*, northern seaoats N
- *Glyceria maxima* 'Variegata', variegated manna grass
- *Hierochloe odorata*, sweetgrass N
- *Juncus effusus*, common rush N
- *Leymus arenarius*, blue lymegrass
- *Miscanthus* 'Purpurascens', red flame miscanthus
- *Miscanthus sacchariflorus*
- *Panicum virgatum*, switchgrass N
- *Phalaris arundinacea* 'Picta', ribbongrass
- *Phalaris arundinacea* var. *luteo-picta*, yellow ribbongrass
- *Phalaris arundinacea* 'Feesey's Form', Feesey's ribbongrass
- *Spartina pectinata*, cordgrass N
- *Spartina pectinata* 'Aureo-Marginata', variegated cordgrass
- *Zizania aquatica*, wild rice (annual) N

hardy in USDA Zone 3*

- *Arrhenatherum elatius* var. *bulbosum* 'Variegatum', bulbous oatgrass
- *Bouteloua curtipendula*, side oats grama
- *Bouteloua gracilis*, blue grama
- *Bromus inermis* 'Skinner's Gold', Skinner's gold brome
- *Calamagrostis xacutiflora* 'Karl Foerster', 'Karl Foerster' feather reedgrass
- *Calamagrostis brachytricha*, fall blooming reedgrass
- *Calamagrostis xacutiflora* 'Overdam', 'Overdam' reedgrass
- *Carex grayi*, Gray's sedge
- *Carex muskingumensis*, palm sedge
- *Carex flacca*, carnation sedge
- *Deschampsia caespitosa*, tufted hairgrass
- *Festuca glauca* 'Elijah Blue', 'Elijah Blue' fescue
- *Festuca glauca* 'Solling', 'Solling' blue fescue
- *Helictotrichon sempervirens*, blue oatgrass
- *Leymus arenarius*, blue lymegrass
- *Miscanthus sacchariflorus*, silver banner grass
- *Miscanthus* 'Purpurascens', red flame miscanthus
- *Miscanthus sinensis* 'Malpartus', 'Malpartus' miscanthus (survived 5 of 7 winters)

Above: manna grass.
Below: the grass collection at Crookston, MN, zone 3.

N = native to United States

* (-30 to -40 degrees C)

Above: snowline sedge with firefly impatiens. Center: tufted hairgrass. Below: 'Toffee Twist' sedge.

- *Miscanthus sinensis* 'Silberfeder', silverfeather miscanthus (survived 5 of 7 winters)
- *Miscanthus* x 'Giganteus', giant miscanthus (survived 5 of 7 winters)
- *Molinia caerulea* 'Variegata', variegated purple moorgrass
- *Molinia caerulea* ssp. *arundinacea* 'Windspiel,' windplay tall moorgrass
- *Panicum virgatum*, switchgrass
- *Phalaris arundinacea* 'Picta', ribbongrass
- *Phalaris arundinacea* var. *luteo-picta*, yellow ribbongrass
- *Phalaris arundinacea* 'Feesey's Form', Feesey's ribbongrass
- *Schizachyrium scoparium*, little bluestem
- *Sorghastrum nutans*, Indian grass
- *Spartina pectinata*, cordgrass
- *Spartina pectinata* 'Aureo-marginata', variegated cordgrass
- *Spodiopogon sibiricus*, silver spikegrass
- *Sporobolus heterolepis*, prairie dropseed

shady locations

- *Carex species*, most sedges N
- *Chasmanthium latifolium*, northern seaoats N
- *Deschampsia caespitosa*, tufted hairgrass N
- *Hakonechloa macra*, hakone grass
- *Hakonechloa macra*, 'Albo-Striata'
- *Hakonechloa macra*, 'Aureola'

- *Elymus hystrix* var. *hystrix*, eastern bottlebrush N
- *Luzula* species, woodrush N
- *Phalaris arundinacea* 'Picta', ribbongrass
- *Phalaris arundinacea* var. *luteo-picta*, yellow ribbongrass
- *Phalaris arundinacea* 'Feesey's Form', Feesey's ribbongrass

dry shade

- *Carex pensylvania*, Pennsylvania sedge N
- *Festuca glauca* 'Elijah Blue', 'Elijah Blue' fescue (light shade)
- *Festuca* species, fescue, (light shade)
- *Helictotrichon sempervirens*, blue oatgrass (light shade)
- *Phalaris arundinacea*, 'Picta', ribbongrass
- *Phalaris arundinacea* var. *luteo-picta*, yellow ribbongrass
- *Phalaris arundinacea* 'Feesey's Form', Feesey's ribbongrass

grasses for containers

- *Acorus calamus* 'Variegatus', variegated sweet flag
- *Alopecurus pratensis* 'Aureus', yellow foxtail
- *Arrhenatherum elatius* var. *bulbosum* 'Variegatum', bulbous oatgrass
- *Calamagrostis xacutiflora* 'Overdam', 'Overdam' feather reedgrass

- *Calamagrostis xacutiflora* 'Avalanche', 'Avalanche' feather reedgrass
- *Carex conica* 'Variegata', variegated sedge
- *Carex muskingumensis*, palm sedge
- *Carex muskingumensis* 'Little Midge', 'Little Midge' palm sedge
- *Carex muskingumensis* 'Oehme', 'Oehme' palm sedge
- *Carex flagellifera* 'Toffee Twist', 'Toffee Twist' sedge
- *Chasmanthium latifolium*, northern seaoats
- *Festuca glauca* 'Elijah Blue', 'Elijah Blue' fescue
- *Hakonechloa macra*, hakone grass
- *Hakonechloa macra* 'Albo-Striata', striped hakone grass
- *Hakonechloa macra* 'Aureola', golden hakone grass
- *Helictotrichon sempervirens*, blue oatgrass
- *Imperata* 'Red Baron', bloodgrass
- *Miscanthus sinensis* 'Variegata', variegated miscanthus
- *Miscanthus sinensis var. condensatus* 'Caberet', 'Caberet' miscanthus
- *Pennisetum alopecuroides* 'Little Bunny', dwarf fountaingrass
- *Pennisetum glaucum* 'Purple Majesty', 'Purple Majesty' millet
- *Pennisteum setaceum*, crimson fountaingrass
- *Pennisteum setaceum* 'Rubrum', purple fountaingrass

annual grasses in cold climates*

- *Arundo donax* 'Variegata', striped giant reed
- *Carex buchananii*, leatherleaf sedge
- *Carex flagellifera* 'Toffee Twist', 'Toffee Twist' sedge
- *Melinis nerviglumis* 'Pink Crystals'™, rubygrass
- *Milium effusum* 'Aureum', golden wood millet
- *Miscanthus sinensis var. condensatus*, 'Cosmopolitan', 'Cosmopolitan' miscanthus
- *Miscanthus sinensis var. condensatus* 'Caberet', 'Caberet' miscanthus
- *Muhlenbergia capillaris* 'Regal Mist'™, pink muhly
- *Nassella tenuissima*, Mexican feathergrass
- *Pennisetum glaucum* 'Purple Majesty', 'Purple Majesty' millet
- *Pennisetum orientale*, oriental fountaingrass
- *Pennisteum setaceum*, tender or crimson fountaingrass
- *Pennisetum setaceum*, 'Rubrum', purple fountaingrass
- *Pennisetum villosum*, feathertop
- *Saccharum ravennae*, plumegrass, ravennagrass

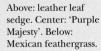

Above: leather leaf sedge. Center: 'Purple Majesty'. Below: Mexican feathergrass.

*(usually annuals in zones 5 and colder)

Above: 'Dallas Blue' switchgrass screens an outdoor patio. Below: feather reedgrass provides a medium height screen.

screens

Screens over 5 feet tall:

❧ *Miscanthus* x 'Giganteus', giant miscanthus

❧ *Miscanthus sinensis* 'Autumn Light', 'Autumn Light' miscanthus

❧ *Miscanthus sinensis* 'Malpartus', 'Malpartus' miscanthus

❧ *Miscanthus sinensis* 'Silberfeder', silverfeather

❧ *Miscanthus sinensis* 'Strictus', porcupinegrass

❧ *Miscanthus sinensis* 'Zebrinus', zebragrass

❧ *Sorghastrum nutans* 'Sioux Blue', 'Sioux Blue' Indian grass

❧ *Panicum virgatum* 'Cloud 9', 'Cloud 9' switchgrass

❧ *Panicum virgatum* 'Dallas Blues', 'Dallas Blues' switchgrass

See-through Screens

❧ *Molinia caerulea* ssp. *arundinacea* 'Skyracer', 'Skyracer' tall moorgrass

❧ *Molinia caerulea* ssp. *arundinacea* 'Transparent', 'Transparent' tall moorgrass

❧ *Molinia caerulea* ssp. *arundinacea* 'Windspiel', 'Windspiel' tall moorgrass

Screens 4-5' tall

❧ *Calamagrostis xacutiflora* 'Karl Foerster', 'Karl Foerster' feather reedgrass

❧ *Miscanthus sinensis* 'Graziella', 'Graziella' miscanthus

❧ *Miscanthus sinensis* 'Klein Fontäne', 'Klein Fontäne' miscanthus

❧ *Panicum virgatum* 'Northwind', 'Northwind' switchgrass

❧ *Spodiopogon sibiricus*, sliver spikegrass

erosion control/ invasive rhizomes

Most ornamental grasses form a dense bunch or clump and do not have invasive rhizomes. The exceptions are listed on page 33 and their ease of propagation and hardiness has led to a misconception that all grasses have creeping roots.

Controlling aggressive rhizomes may be difficult. Be sure you want an aggressive grass before you plant these. Regular edging with a lawn mower, or physical barriers such as blacktop, cement, or other structural confinement can keep these plants in check. Sinking a container in the ground to confine the roots rarely works…the plant roots usually jump out over the top.

In areas where a ground cover is desired or to control erosion on slopes and along lakeshores, invasive rhizomes can be an asset.

- *Carex flacca,* blue sedge
- *Glyceria maxima* 'Variegata', variegated manna grass
- *Hierochloe odorata,* sweetgrass N
- *Leymus arenarius,* blue lymegrass
- *Miscanthus sacchariflorus,* sliver banner grass
- *Phalaris arundinacea* 'Picta', ribbongrass

- *Phalaris arundinacea* var. *luteo-picta,* yellow ribbongrass
- *Phalaris arundinacea* 'Feesey's Form', Feesey's ribbongrass
- *Spartina pectinata,* cordgrass N
- *Spartina pectinata* 'Aureo-Marginata,' variegated cordgrass

grasses that self-seed

It is important to know if a grass will self-seed and become a nuisance in the garden. Native grasses that self-seed usually are not a problem but introduced, non-native plants pose the risk of becoming widespread and dominant if they self-seed. The following grasses have self-seeded in Minnesota growing conditions:

- *Chasmanthium latifolium,* northern seaoats
- *Eragrostis trichodes,* sand lovegrass N
- *Festuca* species, blue fescue
- *Elymus hystrix* var. *hystrix,* eastern bottlebrush N
- *Melica altissima* 'Atropurpurea', red melic
- *Melinis nerviglumis* 'Pink Crystals'™ rubygrass (annual)
- *Miscanthus sinensis* cultivars: two or more cultivars can cross-pollinate and set seed

- *Molinia caerulea* ssp. *arundinacea,* tall purple moorgrass
- *Panicum virgatum,* switchgrass N
- *Pennisetum alopecuroides,* fountain grass
- *Schizachyrium scoparium,* little bluestem N
- *Sorghastrum nutans,* Indian grass N

Above: *Carex flacca* (foreground) and *Leymus arenarius* (back right) have aggressive rhizomes. Below: seedlings of northern seaoats (foreground).

N = native to United States

Above: blue grama. Center and bottom: typical prairie restorations.

hot and dry

Once established, these grasses can withstand drought and hot conditions.

- *Bouteloua curtipendula,* side oats grama N
- *Bouteloua gracilis,* blue grama N
- *Eragrostis trichodes,* sand lovegrass N
- *Festuca glauca,* most cultivars
- *Helictotrichon sempervirens,* blue oatgrass
- *Helictotrichon sempervirens* 'Saphiresprudel', 'Saphiresprudel' oatgrass
- *Imperata* 'Red Baron', bloodgrass
- *Melinis nerviglumis* 'Pink Crystals',™ (annual)

- *Muhlenbergia capillaris,* 'Regal Mist™', pink muhly (annual)
- *Nassella tenuissima,* Mexican feathergrass (annual)
- *Pennisetum orientale,* oriental fountaingrass (annual)
- *Pennisteum setaceum,* tender or crimson fountaingrass (annual)
- *Pennisetum setaceum* 'Rubrum', purple fountaingrass (annual)
- *Pennisetum villosum,* feathertop (annual)

grasses for prairie restoration

Grasses are the backbone of the prairie, throughout the short, mid, and tallgrass prairie. The following native grasses are good choices for prairie restorations and are listed with soil preference. (Mesic soils are medium moisture soils.)

- *Andropogon gerardii*,* big bluestem; mesic to wet soils
- *Bouteloua curtipendula,* side oats grama; dry to mesic soils
- *Bouteloua gracilis,* blue grama; dry soil
- *Buchloe dactyloides,* buffalograss; dry soil
- *Elymus canadensis,* Canada wildrye; mesic soil
- *Koeleria macrantha,* June grass; dry to mesic soils

- *Panicum virgatum*,* switchgrass; wet to mesic soils
- *Schizachyrium scoparium*,* little bluestem; dry to mesic soils
- *Sorghastrum nutans*,* Indian grass; mesic soil
- *Spartina pectinata,* cord grass; wet to mesic soils
- *Sporobolus heterolepis,* prairie dropseed; dry soil

* dominant in the tallgrass prairie

winning combinations

Which plants look good with grasses? We think first of color, but do not forget site and exposure for long-term success. Color combinations are most apparent, but plants that prefer the same soil and site will be winning combinations in your garden for many years. Grey-leaved grasses such as *Helictotrichon* and *Festuca* are typical of sunny, dry conditions; pair these with other drought tolerant perennials such as *Achillea filipendulina* 'Coronation Gold', *Ascelpias tuberosa*, butterfly weed, and *Stachys byzantina*, lamb's ear. Other good combinations include:

* *Arrhenatherum elatius* var. *bulbosum* 'Variegatum' bulbous oatgrass – **with** – *Dianthus deltoides* maiden pinks or *Dianthus* 'Bath's Pink'

* *Calamagrostis xacutiflora* **'Karl Foerster' feather reedgrass – with – roses such as 'Nearly Wild', 'Forever Wild', 'Winnipeg Parks'**

* *Calamagrostis xacutiflora* 'Karl Foerster' feather reedgrass – **with** – *Filipendula rubra*, queen of the prairie

* *Calamagrostis xacutiflora* **'Karl Foerster' feather reedgrass – with – Asiatic lilies**

* *Calamagrostis xacutiflora* 'Overdam', Overdam reedgrass – **with** – *Astilbe xarendsii*, astilbe

* *Carex conica* 'Snowline' ('Variegata'), 'Snowline' sedge – **with** – white *Impatiens walleriana* 'Firefly'

* *Carex siderosticha* 'Variegata', broad leaf sedge – **with** – hot pink or fuchsia flowers such as *Geranium macrorrhizum*

* *Hakonechloa macra* 'Aureola', golden hakone grass – **with** – purple and blue flowers, such as *Iris siberica* 'Lady Vanessa', *Lobelia siphilitica* great blue lobelia, or *Phlox divaricata*, woodland phlox

* *Helictotrichon sempervirens* blue oatgrass with pastel pink and blue flowers such as *XHeucherella* 'Bridget Bloom', *Campanula carpatica* 'Blue Clips'

* *Leymus arenarius* blue lymegrass – **with** – salmon colored flowers such as Zinnia 'Salmon Rose' or 'Dreamland Coral'

* *Miscanthus sinensis* **'Variegatus' variegated miscanthus – with –** *Monarda didyma* **'Raspberry Wine'**

* *Miscanthus sinensis* 'Zebrinus' zebragrass – **with** – yellow daisy flowers such as *Helianthus giganteus*

* *Molinia caerulea* 'Variegata', variegated purple moorgrass – **with** – *Alchemilla mollis*, lady's mantle

* *Sesleria caerulea*, blue moorgrass – **with** – spring flowering bulbs such as *Tulipa* 'Tarda' or *Narcissus* 'Hawera'

* *Schizachyrium scoparium*, little bluestem – **with** – *Aster novea-angeliae* 'Purple Dome'

* *Sporobolus heterolepis*, prairie dropseed – **with** – *Allium cernuum*, nodding onion

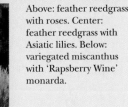

Above: feather reedgrass with roses. Center: feather reedgrass with Asiatic lilies. Below: variegated miscanthus with 'Rapsberry Wine' monarda.

prairie dropseed

alternative lawns

Can ornamental grasses be used to replace a conventional lawn?

Perhaps, but they will not look like the Kentucky bluegrass we are familiar with. Most of the plants listed here cannot tolerate foot traffic (except the fescues and grama grasses), are low-growing, and should be thought of as perennials to make a ground cover instead of a conventional lawn. You may want to try a dozen or so plants in a portion of your yard to see if you like the look.

For large areas in full sun also consider using some of the native prairie grasses listed elsewhere in this publication. Other choices for planting alternative lawns are purchasing grass seed mixes such as "No Mow," or look for fine fescues, usually sold as shady lawn mixes. These fine fescues are excellent choices for sun or light shade areas. Left un-mowed, or mowed once or twice a year, they provide a soft, hay-like look for a more natural lawn. Grass seed and flower mixtures such as 'Ecology Lawn Mix', which contain clover and yarrow are also on the market.

Some maintenance will be required in these alternative lawns, mowing perhaps once or twice a year, mowing or cutting the plants back in early spring, and weeding until plants become fully established. Check local ordinances; some towns prohibit tall grasses (12" or more) in lawns. Small animals, such as mice and gophers as well as birds and snakes, may be attracted to these ground covers, which may be viewed as a positive or negative feature. Grasses more than 3" tall provide attractive cover for field mice and voles. Mowing the edges of a natural meadow, prairie, or alternative lawn will give the element of care, as will adding a water feature, birdbath, birdhouses, or mowed paths.

alternative lawn grasses for sunny locations

- *Bouteloua curtipendula*, side oats grama; 1-2'
- *Bouteloua gracilis*, blue grama; 12-18"
- *Buchloe dactyloides*, buffalograss; 6-12"
- *Carex pensylvanica*, sun sedge; 12-18"
- *Carex flacca*, blue sedge; 6-18"

- *Festuca glauca* 'Elijah Blue', blue fescue; 6-12"
- *Helictotrichon sempervirens*, blue oatgrass; 1-2'
- *Koeleria macrantha*, June grass; 12"
- *Sesleria caerulea*, blue moorgrass; 6-12"
- *Sporobolus heterolepis*, prairie dropseed; 2-3'

prairie dropseed

blue moorgrass

alternative lawn grasses for shady locations

- *Carex* species, most sedges; 6"–2'
- *Deschampsia caespitosa*, tufted hairgrass; 2-4'
- *Hakonechloa macra*, hakone grass; 6-18"
- *Hakonechloa macra* 'Albo-Striata', striped hakone grass; 6-12"

- *Hakonechloa macra* 'Aureola', golden hakone grass; 6-12"
- *Sesleria caerulea*, blue moorgrass; 6-12" (light shade only)

fall color and winter interest

NAME	COMMENTS
Calamagrostis xacutiflora 'Karl Foerster', feather reedgrass	tan foliage, upright form
Calamagrostis brachytricha, fall blooming reedgrass	pink-green fall flowers, tan foliage
Chasmanthium latifolium, northern seaoats	yellow fall color, brown seedheads last all winter
Festuca glauca 'Elijah Blue', 'Elijah Blue' fescue	almost evergreen
Helictotrichon sempervirens, blue oatgrass	almost evergreen
Miscanthus x 'Giganteus', giant miscanthus	tan foliage, winter sound and movement
Miscanthus sinensis, most cultivars	yellow or orange fall color, showy flowers in fall and all winter, usually upright in winter; 'Autumn Light', 'Gracillimus', and 'Morning Light' are the stiffest cultivars
Miscanthus sacchariflorus, silver banner grass	good orange fall color, showy white flowers fall apart in December
Molinia caerulea ssp. *arundinacea*, 'Skyracer', and 'Windspiel', tall purple moorgrass	all tall cultivars are similar in fall: yellow stems and foliage, usuall become prostrate with snow
Panicum virgatum, switchgrass	tan foliage, upright form in winter
Schizachyrium scoparium, little bluestem	orange fall and winter color, silvery fall flowers
Sesleria caerulea, blue moorgrass	almost evergreen
Sorghastrum nutans, Indian grass	yellow and orange fall color, upright attractive flowers in winter
Spartina pectinata, cordgrass	yellow fall color
Spartina pectinata 'Aureo-Marginata', variegated cordgrass	yellow fall color
Spodiopogon sibiricus, silver spike grass	orange, red and bronze fall color; prostrate in winter
Sporobolus heterolepis, prairie dropseed	orange fall color

Above left: switchgrass in winter. Above right: fescue, feather reedgrass and silver spike grass in fall. Below left: feather reedgrass in fall. Below right: miscanthus in winter.

further information

Darke, R. 1999. *The Color Encyclopedia of Ornamental Grasses.* Timber Press. Portland, OR

Foerster, K. 1982. *Einzug der Graeser und Farne in die Gaerten.* Melsunger, E. Verlag J. Neumann-Neudamn. Germany.

Gilsenan, F. and Sunset Books. 2002. *Landscaping with Ornamental Grasses.* Sunset Books, Menlo Park, CA.

Gould, F. and R. Shaw. 1983. *Grass Systematics,* second edition, by L. Gould and R. Shaw. Texas A&M University Press, College Station, TX.

Greenlee, J. 1992. *The Encyclopedia of Ornamental Grasses.* Rodale Press. Emmaus, PA.

Hitchcock, A. S. 1950. *Manual of the Grasses of the United States.* Revised by A. Chase. Government Printing Office, Washington, D.C.

Meyer, M. Hockenberry. 1975. *Ornamental Grasses.* Charles Scribner's Sons. New York.

Oehme, W. and J. Van Sweden. 1990. *Bold Romantic Gardens.* Acropolis Books, Reston, VA.

Ondra, N. 2002. *Grasses: Versatile Partners for Uncommon Garden Design.* Storey Books. North Adams, MA.

Packard, S. and C. Mutel. 1997. *The Tallgrass Restoration Handbook.* Island Press. Washington, D.C.

organizations

Ornamental Grass Society
www.ornamentalgrasssociety.org
P.O. 11144
St. Paul, MN 55111-0144
612-729-1573

sources

Local garden centers and nurseries are a good source for purchasing ornamental grasses. Purchasing plants in a container means a well-developed root system and in the case of native plants, may be adapted to local growing conditions. Mail order sources may supply smaller, unadapted bare root plants, but offer a wider variety. Below is a partial list is sources; it is given for convenience only and does not constitute an endorsement. A good reference for more sources is the Andersen Horticultural Library's Source List of Plants and Seeds, 6th edition, 2004 edited by Richard Isaacson, Anderson Horticultural Library, Chaska, MN.

Ambergate Gardens
8730 County Rd. 43
Chaska, MN 55318-9358
(952) 443-2248
www.ambergategardens.com

American Ornamental Perennials
29644 SE Weitz Lane
Eagle Creek, OR 97022
(wholesale only)
(503) 637-3095
www.gramineae.com

Bailey Nurseries, Inc.
1325 Bailey Road
St. Paul, MN 55119
(wholesale only)
(651) 459-9744
www.baileynursery.com

Bluebird Nursery, Inc.
P.O. Box 460
519 Bryan St.
Clarkson, NE 68629
(wholesale only)
(402) 892-3457
www.bluebirdnursery.com

Kurt Bluemel, Inc.
2740 Greene Lane
Baldwin, MD 21013
(wholesale only)
(410) 557-7229
www.kurtbluemel.com

Bluemount Nurseries, Inc.
2103 Blue Mount Road
Monkton, MD 21111
(410) 329-6226
www.bluemount.com

Busse Gardens
17160 245th Ave. NW
Big Lake, MN 55309
(800) 544-3192
www.bussegardens.com

Earthly Pursuits, Inc.
2901 Kuntz Road
Baltimore, MD 21244
410- 496-2523
www.earthlypursuits.net

Glacial Stone Nursery
N5578 County Rd D
Leopolis, WI 54948
(wholesale only)
715-787-4373
www.glacialstone.com

Greenlee Nursery
257 E. Franklin Ave.
Pomona, CA 91766
909-623-9045
www.greenleenursery.com

Landscape Alternatives
1705 St. Albans St. N
Roseville, MN 55113
651-488-3142
landscapealt@earthlink.net

Limerock Ornamental Grasses
70 Sawmill Rd
Port Matilda, PA 16870
(814) 692 2272
www.limerockgrasses.com

Morning Sky Greenery
44804 East Highway 28
Morris, MN 56267
(320) 392-5282
www.morningskygreenery.com

Plant Delights Nursery
9241 Sauls Road
Raleigh, NC 27603
(919) 772- 4794
www.plantdelights.com

Prairie Future Seed Co.
P. O. Box 644
Menomonee Falls, WI 53052-0644
262-820-0221
pfsco@exec.com

Prairie Moon Nursery
31837 Bur Oak Lane
Winona, MN 55987
(507) 452- 1362
www.prairiemoon.com

Prairie Nursery
P.O. Box 306
Westfield, WI 53964
(608) 296-3679
www.prairienursery.com

Prairie Restorations
P.O. Box 327
Princeton, MN 55371
(763) 389-4342
www.prairieresto.com

Prairie Ridge Nursery
9738 Overland Road
Mount Horeb, WI 53572-2832
(608) 437-5245
www.prairieridgenursery.com

Rice Creek Gardens, Inc.
11506 Highway 65
Blaine, MN 55434
(763) 754-8090
www.ricecreekgardens.com

Sheyenne Gardens
17010-29th St. SE
Harwood, ND 58042
(701) 282-0050